John Clare, The Trespasser

John Goodridge and
R.K.R. Thornton

what terryfying rascals these wood keepers & gamekeepers
are they make a prison of the forrests & are its joalers
(John Clare)

Through the old trapdoor of English law
Mad John they made a trespasser of you
(Chris Wood)

John Clare, The Trespasser

John Goodridge
and R.K.R. Thornton

Five Leaves Publications
www.fiveleaves.co.uk

John Clare, The Trespasser
by John Goodridge and R.K.R. Thornton

Published in 2016 by Five Leaves Publications
14a Long Row, Nottingham NG1 2DH
www.fiveleavesbookshop.co.uk

ISBN: 978-1-910170-29-8

Designed and typeset by Five Leaves

Printed in Great Britain

Contents

For Greg Crossan (1950–2015)

Greg Crossan.

Thornton.

Preface

How does a poet like John Clare hold the interest of generations of poetry lovers? What is it about his poetry that makes it seem so strong and right, and at the same time so clear and transparent? Is it his intimate knowledge of the countryside, the accuracy of his observations, the fluency of his rhythms? It is all of these, but Clare's power derives, we argue, from a deeply metaphorical understanding of the world. This ties his poems together in an intricate web, of which even he may not always have been entirely aware, though we regard him as a highly conscious artist. This web of ideas and images gives the poems a wonderful coherence and effectiveness that draws in generation after generation of readers and admirers.

In this short study we aim to show something of how these complex and understated patterns work, by looking closely at a subject that occupied Clare's mind from the outset of his poetic career: trespass. Clare had good reason to care about trespass, living as he did at a time of intensified land enclosure and what has been called a 'sort of civil war' in the countryside between labourers and gamekeepers, and when customary rights were under attack as never before, including what we would now call the right to roam, so important to Clare. Familiar patterns of village and rural life from Clare's childhood were fast disappearing, and it became his life's work to record his world and these changes, in his poetry and prose.

Our study was first published as an extended chapter of *John Clare in Context*, a book of essays edited by Hugh Haughton, Adam Phillips and Geoffrey Summerfield (Cambridge University Press, 1994). Some materials from the original essay, including the discussion of enclosure and detailed analysis of 'The Mores', have been drawn on in John Goodridge's recent book *John Clare and Community* (Cambridge University Press, 2013, 2015). The present edition of the essay, prepared from a pre-publication typescript, has been extensively revised and corrected, with some new materials and a few new references added, and the primary referencing updated.

We quote from the standard modern editions of Clare, which as far as possible preserve the individualistic spelling and punctuation of his manuscripts, and for those unfamiliar with Clare this takes some getting used to. At the end of the book we include a basic guide to further reading and general sources on Clare, which starts with a summary of editions that we hope will be especially useful for those who are new to Clare's poetry.

We are grateful to our many friends in the Clare community; to those who offered help with or commentary on the essay's earlier incarnation, including Professor Roger Sales, whose enthusiastic response encouraged us to revisit the project; and to Dr Robert Heyes, for kindly checking the manuscript with his usually diligence and deep knowledge of Clare. Any remaining errors are of course our own. Our special thanks are due to the late Peter Moyse, ARPS, for the cover image and other photographs taken in Clare country.

John Goodridge and R.K.R. Thornton, September 2015

johnagoodridge@googlemail.com
rkrthornton@btinternet.com

Illustrations

1. Climbing over the wall

The English poet John Clare (1793-1864) was about thirteen when he first glimpsed 'a fragment' of James Thomson's then-popular poem *The Seasons*. Within days he had bought his own copy of the poem and, in order to read it unobserved, climbed over a wall into a private estate, Burghley Park. Afterwards he composed a poem of his own and for the first time wrote it down. In his autobiographical *Sketches in the Life of John Clare* (1821) he describes this important episode in his life:

> this summer I met with a fragment of Thompsons Seasons a young man, by trade a weaver, much older then myself, then in the village, show'd it me I knew nothing of blank verse nor ryhme either otherwise than by the trash of Ballad Singers, but I still remember my sensations in reading the opening of Spring I cant say the reason, but the following lines made my heart twitter with joy.
>
> > Come gentle Spring, ethereal mildness come
> > And from the bosom of yon dropping cloud
> > While music wakes around, veild in a shower
> > Of shadowing roses, on our plains desend
>
> I greedily read over all I coud before I returnd it and resolvd to posses one my self, the price of it being only 1ˢ/6ᵈ.

It would take careful manoeuvring, at home and at work, and two trips on foot to Stamford, for Clare to get his prize and satisfy the hunger that had awoken in him:

On the next Sunday I started to stamford to buy Thompson, for I teazd my father out of the 1^s/6^d and woud not let him have any peace till he consented to give it me, but when I got there I was told by a young shop boy in the street who had a book in his hand which I found to be 'Collins Odes and poems' that the booksellers woud not open the shop on a Sunday this was a dissapointment most strongly felt and I returned home in very low spirits, but haveing to tend horses the next week in company with other boys I plannd a scheme in secret to obtain my wishes by stelth, giving one of the boys a penny to keep my horses in my absence, with an additional penny to keep the Secret I started off and as we was generally soon with getteing out our horses that they might fill themselves before the flyes was out I got to Stamford I dare say before a door had been opend and I loiterd about the town for hours ere I coud obtain my wishes I at length got it with an agreeable dissapointment in return for my first, buying it for 6^d less then I had propos'd and never was I more pleasd with a bargain then I was with this shilling purchase On my return the Sun got up and it was a beautiful morning I coud not wait till I got back without reading it and as I did not like to let any body see me reading on the road of a working day I clumb over the wall into Burghly Park and nestled in a lawn at the wall side the Scenery around me was uncommonly beautiful at that time of the year and what with reading the book and beholding the beautys of artful nature in the park I got into a strain of descriptive ryhming on my journey home this was 'the morning walk' the first thing I commited to paper[1]

Clare's initiation into literature involves both a literal and a metaphorical trespass. As he climbs into the world of literature, so he also climbs into the private land of the aristocracy. This is a key moment for Clare, one that crystallises a number of basic issues in his life and in his writing. He climbs the wall into Burghley Park to read in peace and avoid the detection of a perceived transgression, 'reading on the road of a working day'. But he is also, consciously or not, completing his act of subversion, which is a three-fold trespass on the time, culture and land of his social superiors. It is a small step for John Clare the truant farmboy, a giant leap forward for John Clare the poet. Once he has climbed over the wall and can wander freely in the pastoral landscape of Burghley Park, and the pastoral poetry of Thomson's *Seasons*, Clare feels sufficiently released from the bondage of class and economic necessity to write down a poem himself, something he says he has never done before.[2] It is as though he has moved into a different life, a world apart from that of a working villager. He has bought his first book and written down his first poem, and the trespass into Burghley stands as a rite of passage, marking his entry into the brave new world of literature.[3]

Of course it could be seen as simply instinctive or expedient for Clare to climb over the wall to read, but the context in which he sets the scene suggests that it is part of a series of ideas and images of trespass that are closely associated in his mind. In the opening pages of the autobiography in which this unusual adventure is set, Clare graphically describes the cultural environment of Helpstone (nowadays spelled 'Helpston'), the 'gloomy village in Northamptonshire, on the brink of the Lincolnshire fens' where he grew up, and where a love of books was thought to be 'a sure indication of laziness', book-reading fit only for 'quallyfiing an idiot for a workhouse'. His parents were, so he claims, 'illiterate to the last degree', and his mother thought higher learning was 'the blackest arts of witchcraft'. His father made him a 'light' child-sized threshing flail and taught him early that his legacy was to be 'the hardship which adam and Eve inflicted on their childern by their inexperienced misdeeds'. Clare exaggerates some of the detail, such as his parent's illiteracy. His father could certainly read, and by Clare's own testimony his mother always hoped her son might be a scholar. And what was a weaver doing with a copy of Thomson's *Seasons*, or a Stamford shop boy with William Collins's *Odes and Poems* in his hand, if books were so rare and so shunned by working people? These two kindred spirits in the story would seem to suggest that Clare was not alone in his venture, and may reflect the beginnings of the heroic struggle for self-improvement and knowledge that would characterise Victorian and later working-class culture. But the general sense of cultural deprivation in Clare's world is nevertheless clear enough. He is a sickly child, 'of a waukly constitution', and he defines himself by his early attempts to acquire learning and culture, wandering off on his own, tracing the strange hieroglyphics of geometry on barn walls, talking to himself. His fellow villagers are quick to recognise these strange moves as the telltale 'symtoms of lunacy', and the boy is marked as an outsider, probably destined for a bad end.

The one cultural area in which the young Clare does not feel alienated is that of popular literature, the 'supersti[ti]ous tales that are hawked about a sheet for a penny', the hundred ballads his father boasts he can sing or recite over his horn of ale in the Blue Bell public house next door, the 'Jiants, Hobbgoblins, and faireys' in the tales that beguiled his childhood fieldwork in the company of old women, and the 'Sixpenny Romances of "Cinderella", "Little Red Riding Hood", "Jack and the bean Stalk", "Zig Zag", "Prince Cherry", etc etc etc', of which he 'firmly believed every page I read and considerd I possesd in these the chief learning and literature of the country'.

So it is very striking that when he describes how he stumbles on official literary culture, in the passage under consideration, Clare uncharacteristically rounds on the 'trash of Ballad singers', perhaps angry at having been led to believe that this kind of verse was all there was. He sets off as soon as he can to consolidate his engagement with the new, literary culture, but discovers very quickly that the boundaries of culture are imposed, not just from within the community, but also from the outside. The bookshop is closed on a Sunday, the one day on which a farmboy might be free to visit it, and the conclusion that bookshops are not for working people seems inescapable.[4] This, as he says, is 'a dissapointment most strongly felt', but Clare hardly pauses, and in the same sentence is describing his plan to 'obtain my wishes by stelth'. There can be no turning back, no matter how strongly fenced off literary culture might seem to be. Further transgressions follow thick and fast. We see Clare stealing time from his employer, bribing his workmate, sneaking off to Stamford at the crack of dawn, 'loiter[ing] about the town' and, finally, getting himself a bargain.

All this prepares us well for the moment when Clare scales the wall into Burghley Park. That action is immediately prompted by his hunger to read the book, and by anxious guilt.

These have been sub-texts throughout, signalled in Clare's ambiguous language. The phrase 'loiterd about the town' suggests both the pleasure and guilt of idleness. An 'agreeable dissapointment' actually means a pleasant surprise, but mixed feelings, as much as the lack of a precise English word for the opposite of 'disappointment', seem to inform the phrase. Having stolen time and bribed a workmate to get his piece of elite culture, he must guiltily hide his pleasure in it. 'I did not like to let any body see me reading on the road of a working day',[5] Clare admits, for if bookshops are not for labourers, neither is reading, at least not on a day when he should be working. His 'trespass' against a culture that seems tacitly forbidden threatens to compound his 'trespass' against his employer's time. There seems only one thing left to do, and that is to go even further down the primrose path, by making a literal, land trespass.

So Clare's incursion into Burghley, like the famous boat-stealing episode in the first book of William Wordsworth's great autobiographical poem *The Prelude*, is 'an act of stealth / And troubled pleasure'.[6] It is also a symbolic act, and signals that to be what Clare became that day, a poet, he must transgress.[7] In order to 'trespass upon parnuss'[8] (i.e. Mount Parnassus, the poets' mountain of ancient Greece), as he later puts it, he would have to cross social, economic, literary and land boundaries. One might say that his whole life would become a sort of trespass. And so trespass imagery, considered in the broad sense of boundaries and those who break or challenge them, pervades John Clare's writings. The theme is taken up in major subjects such as enclosure and—especially in Northampton General Lunatic Asylum where he spent the last twenty-three years of his life—imprisonment. It informs his lifelong interest in Scotland and in gypsy culture. It may be detected in the way he deals with such diverse subjects as love, identity, the role of the poet, and in his attitude to formal systems such as Linnaean botanical classification, or grammar and punctuation. Clare writes repeatedly of his own confrontations with physical and metaphysical boundaries, and he deploys in his writings a large and motley army of boundary-breakers, trespassers, and other free spirits. They include (in alphabetical order) ants, birds,[9] cattle, discharged soldiers, drinkers, drovers, flies, ghosts, gypsies, herd-boys, horses, mole-catchers, moles, outcasts, poachers, packmen, Robin Hood,[10] schoolchildren, Scots, sheep, shepherds, tramps, traders, weeds and the wind, plus of course the poet himself, in numerous guises.

It would obviously not be possible to examine here all the many kinds of trespass experience in Clare's writings; nor can we consider more than a few of Clare's battalions of trespassers. We therefore concentrate in what follows on a few representative areas of the subject. First we follow Clare on a further visit to Burghley Park, the important site for the trespass Clare used to help define and create himself as a poet. We then consider some of the poet's responses to boundaries, to several kinds of trespassers, and finally to land enclosure. Clare is seen to have a complex range of responses to the idea of trespass. He can be awed, afraid, angry at both his trespass and the boundaries that compel him to trespass, yet also willing to announce the trespass and deal with it in a way that uses poetry to transform feelings of guilt and anxiety. As with other areas of his writing, it is Clare's gift to be able to turn threatening realities into art.

2. The road to Burghley Park

Burghley Park was an appropriate place for Clare to begin his new life as a poet. It represented a topographical equivalent to the pictorial landscapes described in his new treasure, *The Seasons*.[11] Its ordered variety, its 'artful nature', inspired him to write poetry, contrasting as it did with the flat landscape outside the walls, which Clare sometimes found oppressive and uninspiring. It is a sort of paradise for him, representing pastoral poetry, inspiration, nature, and the pleasurable—but always fearful and guilty— excitement of being where he knew he should not be.

An early poem, 'Narrative Verses Written after an Excursion from Helpston to Burghley Park' provides an interesting gloss on all this, encapsulating his feelings towards this special place, and confirming its significance to his development as a poet. From Helpston to Burghley Park is not too complicated as a physical journey, but as a symbolic journey it is momentous, from the lowest in the land to almost the highest. Margaret Grainger notes that the journey from Helpston to Burghley is 'Clare's physical journey. But another journey, of mind and spirit, is also taking place in the poem... To enlarge his prospects, literally and metaphorically, he had been forced to venture away from home'.[12]

As with the wall-climbing episode, Clare's first task is to escape from familiar restrictions. He is 'from labour free' (line 5), and is careful to follow a route well-hidden from 'the public view', while protesting—perhaps too much—that a poet's natural love of thickets is the only reason for doing this:

2

O! Joyful morn:—on pleasure bent
    Down thy green slopes and fields I flew
And thro' the thickest covert went
    Which hid me from the public view
Nor was it shame nor was it fear
    No no it was my own dear choise
I love the Brierey thicket where
    Echo keeps her mocking voice[13]

Clare seems aware that this is a special journey, and in the third stanza presents it in terms that remind us of John Bunyan's *The Pilgrim's Progress*: 'I left my own fields far behind / And pilgrim-like trod foreign ground'. The landscape takes on a kind of enhanced reality: 'every wood and field me thought / A greener brighter prospect wore' (stanza 3); and while he notes the absence of sublime scenery ('no hughe rock... Nor lofty mountain', stanza 4), he is able to pursue the poetic activities of wandering and wondering. Preparing for Burghley, he muses on the legacy of ancient history (stanza 6), on memories of reading poetry, naming Robert Bloomfield's volume *Rural Tales* (stanza 7) and on places he passes on the journey (stanzas 8-10). The first allusion to Burghley, in stanza 11, is as both memory and desire, and in the phrase 'ere the oak tree tops appeared', as something glimpsed in the distance. Like Bunyan's heavenly city, Burghley gleams, and as in eighteenth-century poetry the poet's aesthetic pleasure in it is based on its happy mingling of opposites or *concordia discors*:

But O! that spot so long endear'd
 Gleaming rapterous on my sight
Fill'd—ere the oak tree tops appeard
 My Breast with wonder and delight
There art and nature friendly join'd
 Intermingling charm'd the eye
And as their varying forms combin'd
 Each gave each a nobler dye[14]

The power of his 'fancy' provides him with memories of Burghley, and enables him to admire its inspiring contrasts:

Enough thy power—the spacious park
 The towering chasenuts hughe and high
The arching groves and walks so dark
 And all appear in mem'rys eye (stanza 12)

But now, the mood changes, and characteristically, doubts and fears begin to surface. He has reached Burghley in his mind: to reach it in reality will be more difficult. Will he be seen? Will he have enough time? Will he be caught trespassing? Again he has to avoid people, and again this is artfully presented as an aesthetic matter, the need to be the archetypal lonely poet surrounded by nature—though as Clare later admits, it also has much to do with fear of capture, punishment, and ostracism:

13
With deep regret I view'd the spire
 Which told the busy vil so nigh [town or village]

For lonley shades are my desire
  Far from the reach of human eye
The foot pad turning to the town   [footpath]
  No longer provd alone to me
Loud noisy murmurs filld the air
  And spoild my deep sollemnity

The familiar fear of not having enough time spurs him on, and forces an immediate trespass. He quits the pathways and once again finds himself climbing over a wall:

14

The passing hours jog'd on apace
  And in their progress seem'd to say,
'Haste, and gain that destined place
  'Or soon thoult loose the flitting day'
I instantly obey'd their call
  Nor went to where the foot-pad lay
But clamberd oer an old rough wall
  And stole across the nearest way

This time, though, Clare is highly alert to his trespass. This is not Burghley Park, but an unspecified, perhaps more dangerous, more open place to trespass. His fearful consciousness of this danger restricts his ability to read the beauties of the landscape:

15

No spire I caught nor woody swell
  My Eye confind to lower bounds

Yet not to mark the flowrets bell
    But watch the owners of the grounds
Their presence was my only fear
    No boughs to shield me if they came
And soon amid my rash career
    I deemd such trespasing to blame

16

For troubl'd thoughts began to rise
    Of ills almost beyond relief
Which might from this one cause arise
    And leave me there to whant reprief
So arguing with myself how vain
    An afterthought 'Still to keep free'
Made me to seek the road again
    And own the force of Liberty

As these stanzas show, Clare was immensely sensitive to the implications, not only of his own words, but also of meanings that could be imputed to his actions. Perhaps this quality gave rise to his great shyness and his fear of the dark. He was always capable of being spooked by unknown places and experiences. Here he is spooked by his own trespassing and returns to the road to save himself from possible capture by the landowner. There are hints of self-reproach in this confession. He has abandoned his priorities as a poet in favour of naked self-preservation, and the words 'free' and 'Liberty' are ironically paradoxical (staying free by admitting he is not free) as well as confessionally honest.[15] Yet the final word of the stanza, 'Liberty', retains its rhetorical power, and enables Clare to

rescue the memory—and his dignity—from what seems at face
value to be an ignominious retreat:

17

For O! its unabated power
    Did then my breast with raptures fill
And sure it was a happy hour
    That led me up to Barnack hill
There uncontrould I knew no bounds
    But lookt oer Villages a crowd
And cots and spires to farthest rounds
    While far trees seem'd a misty cloud

Clare is able to rescue the situation through his new position on
Barnack Hill, overlooking Burghley from the only commanding
height in the area, whose symbolic significance is enhanced by its
position at the point where Ermine Street enters Burghley Park.[16]
He has now reached his destination, and can perform the ritual
for which he has come to Burghley: to make a wish, inspired by
the scenery and aided by his muse, for success as a pastoral poet:

18

While tir'd with such farstretching views
    I left the green hills sideling slope
But O! so tempting was the muse
    She made me wish she made me hope
I wish'd and hop'd that future days
    (For scenes prophetic fill'd my breast)
Whould grant to me a Crown of bays
    By singing maids and shepherds drest

24

In the final stanzas (19-21) Clare ventures further into Burghley Park, his interior vision (memory, fancy) responding to the exterior visions in the Park: awe-inspiring groves, walks and views and the 'massy grated gate' of the Park (again suggesting themes of trespass and entry). The combination of themes in the poem is noteworthy: literature, poetic ambition and composition, the aristocratic house and park, trespass and freedom, roads and hidden routes. His engagement with the landscape is closely connected with his poetic ambitions. At this stage in his career we can appropriately use eighteenth-century terms to describe these connections: 'prospects' (what he can see, and what his own 'prospects' are); 'decorum' (where one should or should not venture, on the land or in poetry); and 'the sublime', a term of particular relevance to the closing stanzas, in which Clare's fear of being caught trespassing, and his overawed response to the sense of aristocratic control implied by the structures of Burghley Park, are easily translated into a poetic frisson of sublime fear.

Burghley Park here becomes a proving ground and a touchstone for Clare, and the act of trespassing in it—so casual and informal in the *Seasons* episode—is formalised into a solemn, dangerous, ritual act, intimately tied up with becoming a poet. The park encapsulates his greatest hopes and fears as regards both landscape and poetry. It is a place of inspiration, and has to be approached with the zeal of Bunyan's Christian, yet with the guile of an intruder. In a later poem, 'The Progress of Ryhme', it is remembered as a spiritually-inspiring place, the site of a visionary experience which left the young Clare 'itching after ryhme':

Both insects & the breath of flowers
To sing their makers mighty powers
Ive thought so as I used to rove
Through burghley park that darksome grove
Of Limes where twilight lingered grey
Like evening in the midst of day
& felt without a single skill
That instinct that would not be still
To think of song sublime beneath
That heaved my bosom like my breath
That burned & chilled & went & came
Without or uttering or a name
Untill the vision waked with time
& left me itching after ryhme[17]

There are other locations that have similarly intense meaning for Clare. 'Round Oak Waters', 'Swordy Well', 'Emmonsales Heath' and 'Langley Bush', to name four, have become familiar-seeming places to many poetry readers as a result of Clare's intense engagements with them in his poems. But Burghley is especially interesting because it is associated for Clare with important experiences in his development as a poet; and it would accordingly continue to hold a significant place in his poetry.[18] On the one hand, Burghley meant pleasure: enjoyment of its ordered, pastoral landscape; poetic ecstasy in the visionary experiences Clare felt there. On the other hand, there is a strong sense of limitation and anxiety about what he could and could not do there. The question of how far he could go within the literary culture he had discovered is metaphorically suggested by the issue of how far he could go within areas of the physical landscape that were forbidden to him.

The idea of trespass is central to both issues, and the significance of Clare's anxieties about trespassing should not be underestimated. Several passages in his writings suggest not merely anxiety, but a real terror of being caught trespassing. For instance he records in his Journal for Saturday 16 April 1825:

Took a walk in the field a birds nesting and botanizing and had like to have been taken up as a poacher in Hillywood by a meddlesome consieted keeper belonging to Sir John Trollop   he swore that he had seen me in act more then once of shooting game when I never shot even so much as a sparrow in my life—what terryfying rascals these wood keepers and gamekeepers are   they make a prison of the forrests and are its joalers[19]

Clare had good reason to live in terror of the keepers and the trespass and game laws. J.L. and Barbara Hammond, perhaps the most eloquent chroniclers of the subject, record that a 'sort of civil war was going on between the labourers and the gamekeepers' in the period, a view put even more strongly by Harry Hopkins in his book *The Long Affray* (1985). The effects of poverty, exacerbated by wartime and post-war conditions, the agricultural slump of 1815, and the increasingly draconian game laws (the Hammonds describe those of 1770, 1800, 1803, 1816 and 1831, and there were many others), led to greatly increased levels of violence and brutality in this war. Murderous spring guns that could kill or maim were, say the

Hammonds, 'evidently common by 1817'—mantraps had long been familiar. In the years between 1827 and 1831 'one in seven of all criminal convictions in the country were convictions under the Game Code'.[20]

The sources of Clare's fear are not hard to find in the Hammonds' account. Had the gamekeeper who accused him of poaching been believed, Clare could have been sentenced to imprisonment, with the possibility of a public whipping and/or hard labour, or (after 1816) seven years transportation. To give an extreme and admittedly rather unlikely example, had the keeper attempted to arrest Clare and been violently resisted, the poet could have been hanged, under Lord Ellenborough's law of 1803. But then again, should Clare even so much as have broken the branch of a tree while trespassing, he could have been sent to the House of Correction under the Malicious Trespass Act of 1820. The statutory penalties do not necessarily indicate what actually happened in the countryside, but Harry Hopkins's trawl through the sources nets more than enough legally sanctioned brutality for the strongest stomach. There was a strong, resistant sense in the countryside that the game laws were a perversion of natural law. No matter what the penalties, they would continue to be resisted. But we can see how intimidated by these draconian measures Clare would be. His lifelong hatred of prisons and imprisonment clearly stems from real, well-founded fears.[21]

Even Burghley Park itself, Clare's sacred grove, could be turned into an enclosing prison, as it apparently was when Clare worked there as an under-gardener, in his late teens:

I learnt irregular habbits at this place which I had been stranger too had I kept at home   tho we was far from a

28

town yet confinement sweetens liberty and we stole every oppertunity to get over to Stamford on summer evenings... we usd to get out of the window and climb over the high wall of the extensive gardens for we slept in the garden house and was locked in every night to keep us from robbing the fruit I expect—Our place of rendevouse was a public house calld 'the Hole in the wall' famous for strong ale and midnight merriment[22]

The ironically appropriate name of the escapees' meeting place, 'the Hole in the wall', underlines Clare's plight. In order to move freely rules have to be broken, walls breached, risks taken. As with the *Seasons* episode, Clare has to engage in various kinds of subversion and subterfuge. Whether he is escaping as he is here, or breaking in as in the earlier texts quoted, the landscape, and the power structures it embodies, exercise a double psychological control over the poet: the sinister accompaniment to Clare's visionary ecstasy is a darker mood of fear, risk, and circumscription.

3. Land boundaries and the vectors of trespass

The abundance of pleasurable imagery in Clare's descriptive poetry makes it harder for us to conceive of his environment, the countryside that is the major site of his poetry, in terms of fear. Clare himself, for whom poetry is often a haven of optimism and an idealised alternative to the harsh realities of his life, characteristically discourages such a reading. Yet there are, as we have seen, clear suggestions of hostility and threat in Clare's environment. The sonnet-in-couplets that his editors J.W. and Ann Tibble entitled 'Trespass' expresses a kind of horror of breaking the trespass laws, only partly alleviated by the poem's naive appeals to beauty and to the poet's unpropertied innocence:

> I dreaded walking where there was no path
> & prest with cautious tread the meadow swath
> & always turned to look with wary eye
> & always feared the owner coming bye
> Yet everything about where I had gone
> Appeared so beautiful I ventured on
> & when I gained the road where all are free
> I fancied every stranger frowned at me
> & every kinder look appeared to say
> Youve been on trespass in your walk to day
> Ive often thought the day appeared so fine
> How beautiful if such a place were mine
> But having nought I never feel alone
> & cannot use anothers as my own[23]

In his poem 'To John Clare', Neil Philip notes the 'happiest sanity' of Clare's ability to 'start so many poems with the words "I love"'.[24] This is well-observed, and it is curious how unlike Clare's usual tone the first line of the trespass sonnet, 'I dreaded walking where there was no path', seems. We think of him always walking trackless ways. Yet we have to realise how much that was a deliberate, often difficult and dangerous thing to do, how much his imagination conjured up anxieties and dangers. In this poem even the road where 'all are free' offers no relief from fear, imaginary frowns are everywhere, and even the kindness of strangers is felt to somehow mask a silent accusation of transgression and trespass.

One of the results of Clare's pervasive awareness of spatial limitation is that his writings are full of images of land boundaries, and of the main functions of boundaries, to enclose and to exclude, to mark territory and to limit free movement. We find such images in the earliest part of his life, as when the young Clare grapples with the matter of the square on the hypotenuse:

> I Saw a Tree with Cheries Red,
> Whose Height was 40 Foot,
> A Moat against it hinder'd me
> That I could not get to't,
> The Moat was 30 Feet all Wet
> The Question now must be
> How Long a Ladder I must Set
> To reach the Top o' the Tree.[25]

We find them again in his middle years, as when he attempts, in increasing confusion and anger, to sort out his money, in a letter to his publisher John Taylor:

> To mend the fences of safety that guard my domestic benefits without bringing <every> the other matters to a conclusion—would be a vain attempt—it would be only repairing fences where destroying matters had crept in— & hedging them in to destroy more so the best way is to get them out before I begin to mend the outward fence[26]

And inevitably, we find them intensely re-literalised in the writings of Clare's asylum period:

> I love to clamber over these bridge walls & when I get off the banks on the road I instinctively look both ways to see if any passengers are going or coming or carts or waggons passing—now here is a stile partitioning off sombodys portion of the bank but the middle rail is off so I stoop under to get through instead of climbing over it[27]

These three very different examples of boundary images show how pervasively such imagery lodges itself in Clare's thought and language. They also show the way that Clare's thoughts about boundaries habitually move in the direction of getting past them. In the first example, fairy-tale-like with cherries as his imaginary reward, we know, as presumably does Clare, that there is a solution to the riddle, a particular formula for crossing the boundary and getting to the cherry tree. In the middle example a deeply frustrating situation, in which his money seems locked away from him by his trustee, is so problematic as to become almost incommunicable, and his extended metaphor of land boundaries collapses into a semantic muddle of hedge-breaking and hedge-building. (This is an abandoned draft of a letter.)

The third quotation, by contrast, is a classic example of Clare successfully negotiating land boundaries and taking pleasure from doing so. He imagines sizing up the boundary—a wall and a stile, finds the weak spot (the missing middle rail) as instinctively as a mountain climber reaching for a handhold, and slips through it. He then describes what he finds beyond the barrier:

> there is a pair of harrows painted red standing on end against the thorn hedge & in another ground an old plough stands on its beam ends against a dotterel tree sometimes we see a roll lying in on one corner & broken trays & an old gate off the hooks waiting to be repaired till repairs are useless—even these rustic implements & appendages of husbandry blend with nature & look pleasing in the fields[28]

At a time when enormous efforts were being put into farming efficiency and productivity, Clare takes pleasure here in symbols of farming *un*-productivity: the stationary harrow, the old plough, the abandoned roller and perhaps especially the gate off its hooks, a symbol of freedom. In this kind of writing Clare uses trespass and the flouting of boundaries as a way of insisting on a rural aesthetic in which productivity and labour and the orderly landscapes they require are put aside. Even that favourite theme, the coming of Spring, can be symbolised by a broken and decayed hedge, in the poem 'Young Lambs':

> The spring is coming by a many signs
> The trays are up the hedges broken down
> That fenced the haystack & the remnant shines
> Like some old antique fragment weathered brown.
>
> (lines 1-4)[29]

To find this aesthetic in autumn is perhaps less surprising: 'then the Autumn patches of painted wood-nooks with an old gate or broken stile or rails underneath'.[30] There is something of the mainstream pastoral and picturesque traditions here, in which labour is artistically beguiled—made to seem irrelevant, or pleasurable, or something to be carried out by someone else. But Clare's focus on boundaries with its particular emphasis on ways through them, and the pleasure taken in images of broken gates, holes in hedges, and the like, are his own. It brings together a number of his ideas and feelings. In the poem 'Evening Schoolboys', for example, Clare writes:

Where the retiring sun that rests the while
Streams through the broken hedge—How happy seem
Those schoolboy friendships leaning oer the stile[31]

There are several overlapping areas of interest here. Clare is concerned with the way in which the setting sun naturally comes through the break in the hedge. If the break is not exactly a natural phenomenon, it is to some extent restored to this status as compared to an unbroken hedge, through which the sun would not shine. His pleasure in the broken hedge has an aesthetic significance. Does it also gain from the fact that the poet has ideological reasons for liking flaws in hedges? The break is seen as a desirable thing, but the meaning Clare invests in it is channelled into its aesthetics. The stile, the second 'vector' mentioned, is given significance as a meeting place associated with the pleasures of childhood friendship. But the very fact that it is a stile, a route through a boundary, deepens its significance. It is implicitly a route not only to the memory of childhood friendship, but also to whatever landscape lies behind it. It does not much matter what that landscape is in this instance, A stile is by definition a way of getting through a barrier, which for Clare is always an interesting thing to do.

If we cannot easily separate the various impulses feeding into Clare's interest in the vectors of trespass, we can at least understand what they are. Clare's intense dismay at enclosure is reiterated in poem after poem. Thus the poet draws attention, again and again, to a political issue whose presence in the physical world is indicated by fences, hedges, walls and ditches. Given the centrality of this in his work, any mention of a broken hedge will immediately draw the reader's attention to the issue of enclosure, and to Clare's political as well as his aesthetic dislike of a bounded landscape. The poet may be admiring the sun as it shines through a broken hedge, or the way broken gates and stiles 'blend with nature'. He may even be innocently celebrating the daring escape of a fox 'through the hedge' after playing dead:

> & when he rested to his dogs supprise
> The old fox started from his dead disguise
> & while the dog lay panting in the sedge
> He up & snapt and bolted through the hedge[32]

But he is also, in these and many other such moments in his writings, exploring questions of enclosure and trespass, probing the weaknesses and limits of a parcelled-up landscape, developing fantasies of penetration and escape, and rehearsing in poetry a world without the 'hated sign' that says 'no road here'.[33] This does not take anything away from whatever else he is doing in these texts. It ought, however, to warn us against the critical tradition that Clare is a transparently descriptive poet, not in any deep sense metaphorical or aware of wider implications. The theme of trespass does not simply reflect a personal, nostalgic reaction against the enclosure of Helpstone, but is also a way for Clare to explore, in a broader sense, the politics of landscape, and the ideology and psychology of human boundedness and freedom. He examines these subjects through his own experiences, but wider implications are not hard to find when we follow a theme like trespass through Clare's writings.

4. Gypsies, Scottish drovers and other Clarean trespassers

Clare's explorations of trespass and trespass-related subjects are sometimes direct and sometimes presented as subtle sub-texts. Literal and metaphorical, social and psychological trespasses are intertwined. Some of the most powerful writing on these themes is autobiographical, as in the Burghley Park texts we looked at earlier. But trespass for Clare is not always a personal matter, not just a solitary, fearful game of hide-and-seek with gamekeepers and landowners. Although he often saw himself as an isolated figure, Clare had a number of allies who, if they did not always share his literary concerns, could certainly share his love of roaming free. Here we look at some examples of such trespassers, in particular, gypsies and Scottish drovers.

Gypsies are much the most important human trespassers in Clare's writing, apart from the poet himself. They were natural allies, unlike the static, alien breed of Wordsworth's poem 'Gipsies'. For Clare they were companions during Sunday escapes, receivers and sharers of peas stolen from the fields.[35] They were fellow music-lovers who taught him to play the fiddle.[36] They helped him to escape from High Beech, the first asylum, where he lived from 1837-41.[37] Gypsies were, so to speak, natural trespassers, their whole way of life based on a counter-cultural refusal of the ideology of private property. Clare paints an idyllic picture of their lives in a 'Song', first published anonymously in the *European Magazine* in 1825:

> The gipseys life is a merry life
> & happy boys we be
> We pay no rent nor tax to none
> But live untythd & free
> None cares for us for none care we
> & w[h]ere we list we roam
> & merry boys we gipseys be
> Tho the wild woods are our home (lines 1-8)[38]

As this suggests, gypsies were regular users of common land, maintaining and epitomising its status as a sanctuary in an increasingly closed down landscape, in the way modern ramblers keep footpaths open by walking them regularly. As Clare writes in *The Shepherd's Calendar*:

> In such lone spots these wild wood roamers dwell
> On commons w[h]ere no farmers claims appear
> Nor tyrant justice rides to interfere[39]

They were also outsiders, and Clare had from his earliest writings seen himself in an outsiderly role, wandering in the woods and fields alone. The alienated poet-figure of Gray's *Elegy*, a text constantly echoed in Clare's early poems, provided him with one model. But Clare could only go so far along the road of solitary isolationism. In the company of equals he was a naturally sociable man, and the great attraction of the gypsy lifestyle, as Clare's descriptions of it make clear, is its sociability.[40] Here one could be an outsider without the tragic sense of isolation felt by Thomas Gray's lonely poet-figure. This was a genuinely alternative society, which Clare, with his particular priorities and sensibilities, could not but admire and engage in.

So if he travelled to Burghley to enlarge his 'prospects' in one way, he visited the gypsies to do so in another way, for instance by consulting a gypsy fortune-teller:

> Oft on my hand her magic coins bin struck
> & hoping chink she talkd of morts of luck
> & still my boyish hopes did erst agree
> Mingld wi fears to drop the fortunes fee
> I never faild to gain the honours sought
> & Lord & Squire was purchasd wi a groat[41]

Clare is wisely sceptical about how the gypsy fortune-teller effectively offers him the chance to 'purchase' his way into the freedoms of the aristocracy 'for a groat'. But he is also intrigued, and it is evident that he is fascinated by all aspects of gypsy culture. Like broken gates and gaps in hedges, gypsies enhance the appearance of the landscape. He is quite clear about this: 'I thought the gipseys camp by the green wood side a picturesque and an adorning object to nature and I lovd the gipseys for the beautys which they added to the landscape'.[42] Clare is aware that his is not the only view—he characterises gypsies elsewhere as 'poor ragd out casts of the land', and 'A quiet, pilfering, unprotected race'.[43] But against the prejudiced view of gypsies as intruders, he casts them as natural intimates of the landscape, in tune with its mysteries:

> They know the woods & every foxes den
> & get their livings far away from men

> The shooters ask them where to find the game
> The rabbits know them & are almost tame.
> The aged woman tawney with the smoke
> Go with the winds & crack the rotten oak.[44]

When village boys hunt rabbits, it is a gypsy boy who initiates them into the arts of digging out rabbits and training dogs:

> When any comes they skulk behind the tree
> The gipsy joins them in his rage & glee
> & digs the holes out with a rotten stake
> & thrusts his hand & never cares for snakes
> The dog that follows all that passes bye
> He ties him to his hand & makes him lie[45]

Gypsy girls, on the other hand, are admired in a different way. Clare writes of 'The beautiful gipsey with brown swarthy cheek / And a bosom of snow melting under her gown'.[46] The exotic 'otherness' of gypsies is eroticised, in the convention of the gypsy ballad. One could read a number of Clare's poetic responses to trespass and to land boundaries in sexual terms. If such responses are usually either conventionalised, as here, or available only as a covert sub-text, this may reflect the heavy moral scrutiny that afflicted writers in this period, especially writers like Clare and Keats who were perceived as being of a lower social class.[47]

If gypsies are read by Clare as being what we have called 'natural' trespassers, they also trespass in specific ways. In Clare's poem addressed to 'Langley Bush', for example, their search for firewood has a second effect:

> thou art reverenced even the rude clan
> Of lawless gipseys drove from stage to stage
> Pilfering the hedges of the husband man
> Leave thee as sacred in thy withering age
> Both swains and gipseys seem to love thy name
> Thy spots a favourite with the smutty crew
> & soon thou must depend on gipsey fame[48]

Behind the negative implication of words like 'lawless' and 'pilfering' one glimpses a thinning hedge, increasingly be-gapped and therefore, as we have seen, of considerable interest to the poet, and Clare refers elsewhere to 'gaps the gypsey pilfers thin'.[49]

It would be incautious for the poet to be too positive about gypsy firewood-stealing and boundary-breaking, however, and the only mitigation this passage can overtly offer for the behaviour of the 'smutty crew' is the gypsies' reverential skirting of Langley Bush as a site for gathering firewood.[50] In the opening decades of the nineteenth century 'pilfering' anything in the countryside was solidly discouraged by laws and heavy social pressures—fences of an ideological and penal kind to reinforce the physical ones the gypsies liked to thin out a bit to get firewood. Yet for a writer, genre can often find ways to cross such ideological barriers, and poetry itself can offer a transformed version of the real world. Clare feels no restriction, for example, preventing him from channeling rural pilfering and boundary-breaking into the safety of a comic and sentimental eulogy on a favourite horse. Farm animals are not subject to moralising pressures, even if they have learned their tricks from the gypsies, as has the horse 'Dobbin' in the poem 'Going to the Fair':

When loose from geers he roved as freedoms mate
Hed find all gaps & open every gate
& if aught sweet beyond his pasture grew
No fence so thick but he would blunder thro'
His youth from gipseys did these tricks recieve
With them he toiled & worked his wits to live
Bare roads he traced all day with nought to bite
Then stole with them to stacks to feed at night
Tho now a better life was Dobbins lot
Well fed & fat youths tricks he neer forgot
Still gaps were broke & Dobbin bore the blame
Still stacks were pulled & Dobbin felt no shame[51]

This is almost a condensed guide to Clarean trespass: three
ways to get through a fence (find the gaps, open the gate, or
simply blunder through), gypsies and animals together finding
paths to freedom, a humorous echo of the proverb about the
grass always being greener (or in this case sweeter) on the other

side, an appropriate pun on 'stole', subversive trickery and 'wits', freedom from 'shame', and a comic turning upside down of the orderly rural world of fences and haystacks. It says it all, really.

Most importantly, 'Dobbin' allows Clare to celebrate gypsy freedoms without ideological hesitancy of the sort we can detect in the language of 'Langley Bush'. The evidence of Clare's own writings is that gypsies and other trespassers would be dangerous allies for him to embrace. Among the prose materials on gypsies collected together in his autobiographical writings, for example, Clare quotes a Justice of the Peace whose ferocious view is that 'This atrosious tribe of wandering vagabonds ought to be made outlaws in every civilizd kingdom and exterminated from the face of the earth'.[52] Clare roundly condemns this quasi-fascistic viewpoint, but one can well understand how the power of such men represented a very real threat to Clare's propensity towards wandering and associating with gypsies. His fear of being taken as a trespasser or a poacher is ultimately a fear of the magistrate before whom he would be taken. On one occasion Clare describes a sinister incident in which as a celebrated 'peasant poet', he is taken out for the day by a magistrate, who attempts to involve him in catching a phantom 'poacher', dreamed up by the magistrate on the basis of a labourer's innocent whistling:

he took me with him to see Falkingham joal a good distance from Morton and everyone we met gentle or simple he woud stop to speak too and almost ask their business nay he woud question those that appeard his inferiors as if they were under going an examination in a court of justice—once when we were going to see

45

Belvoir Castle while walking by a plantation a labourer happend to break out into a brisk loud whistle of a song tune and he instantly stopt to listen and swore they were poachers and bade me go on the other side to watch which way they started   I tryd to convince him that the whistle was a song tune but it was no use—and as soon as the fellow heard or perhaps saw that he was suspected tho hid from us I expect he felt fearful he stopt his whistle   this convinced the other that his opinion was right—so after watching awhile the fellow made his appearance and met us to know if we was waiting for him   He askd him his business there and he said he was putting down fencing which satisfied the magistrate— who I verily believe mistrusted every stranger for thieves and vagabonds[53]

Clearly the paranoia in the countryside at this time was not just a product of Clare's sensitive imagination. Everything about this incident signals the magistrate's urge to exercise control over others. He has dragged Clare away from the harvest, shown him a prison, and spent the rest of the day demonstrating his officious desire to make everyone explain themselves to him. The language ('joal', 'gentle or simple' i.e. upper or lower class, 'his inferiors', 'poachers', 'thieves and vagabonds') shows that Clare is aware this man is powerful, intensely class-conscious, and dangerous. This does not prevent the poet from capturing the various ironies of the situation through his fine observation of details: that the magistrate should want him—of all people—to be impressed by a gaol (Clare loathed prisons); that a 'song' should be

evidence of criminality (Clare famously wrote of his own 'right to song' as a lyric poet[54]); and that the labourer's 'putting down fencing'—i.e. constructing a land barrier—should have finally 'satisfied' the magistrate.

To befriend gypsies would seriously provoke such men. Not surprisingly, Clare's writings often err on the side of caution, rendering gypsies safe by figuring them within acceptable literary conventions of the picturesque, the comic, the sentimental or the exotic, or else employing the kind of orthodox terminology we saw in 'Langley Bush'. This is not always the case, however. In the group of prose passages on gypsies in his autobiographical writings, and in the gypsy passage in the poem 'The Village Minstrel' (stanzas 113-17) there is a more documentary approach to the subject. No emotional appeal is needed to mitigate the fact that gypsies trespass and steal firewood when we learn that need drives them to eat diseased sheep carcasses, or 'any nauceaous thing their frowning fates provide' ('The Village Minstrel', stanza 114). In such texts Clare repeatedly brings together hardship and law-breaking in this kind of way. The reader is made to look afresh at gypsies not merely as interesting exotics, but as fellow-mortals driven by familiar needs and contingencies, and particularly vulnerable to the hardship of rural life.

Clare's Scottish drovers, on the other hand, appear in an almost entirely romantic aspect. The poet's pervasive 'Scottishness' is striking, and has a number of sources. He had a Scottish grandfather, the itinerant schoolmaster John Donald Parker who left behind his son, Clare's father, as 'one of fates chance-lings who drop into the world without the honour of matrimony'.[55] Clare took a keen interest in the Scottish ballad tradition and in the writings of Burns, Cunningham, Fergusson, Hogg, Ramsay, Scott and Tannahill. It may be significant that all but one of these seven writers were from humble backgrounds.[56] Clare could turn out an authentic-sounding Scottish ballad with extraordinary facility when the mood took him—which was often—and expressed in his poems romantic yearnings for a country he would never see.

Part of the explanation may lie in Clare's experience of Scottish drovers, and in the freedom he associated with them and their native land. Unlike gypsies, drovers are not a common presence in Clare's writings, but where they do appear, in *The Shepherd's Calendar*, their presence is powerful:

> Along the roads in passing crowds
> Followd by dust like smoaking clouds
> Scotch droves of beast a little breed
> In swelterd weary mood proceed
> A patient race from scottish hills
> To fatten by our pasture rills
> Lean wi the wants of mountain soil

But short & stout for travels toil
Wi cockd up horns & curling crown
& dewlap bosom hanging down
Followd by slowly pacing swains
Wild to our rushy flats & plains
At whom the shepherds dog will rise
& shake himself & in supprise
Draws back & waffles in affright
Barking the traveller out of sight
& mowers oer their scythes will bear
Upon their uncooth dress to stare
& shepherds as they trample bye
Leaves oer their hooks a wondering eye
To witness men so oddly clad
In petticoats of banded plad
Wi blankets oer their shoulders slung
To camp at night the fields among
When they for rest on commons stop
& blue cap like a stocking top
Cockt oer their faces summer brown
Wi scarlet tazzeles on the crown
Rude patterns of the thistle flower
Unbrinkd & open to the shower
& honest faces frank & free
That breath of mountain liberty[57]

The staring mower and the barking shepherd's dog, accustomed to the territorial orderliness of their own bounded landscape, seem amazed and perhaps even threatened by the free-ranging character of the Scottish men, their beasts, and their appearance and demeanour. For the drovers, like the gypsies, are exotic strangers who wander freely and enjoy a night-time, camp-fire culture. There is ample evidence in Clare's writings that being abroad at night is in itself transgressive.[58]

The drovers' clothing catches his eye, with the strange freedoms suggested by their 'petticoats of banded plad' (i.e. kilts), and their 'blankets' casually slung over their shoulders. The 'scarlet tazzeles' they like to sport on their caps would seem especially romantic to Clare, who tells elsewhere of childhood searches for red and blue flowers to make cockades for playing soldiers. In a later poem Clare specifically draws together romantic battles and romantic ballads: 'Scotland I love thy every scene / Thy Bannockburn and Bonny Jean'.[59] The drovers are brown-faced like the gypsies. They rest on common land and camp in the fields. And they have 'honest faces frank & free / That breath of mountain liberty'. This clearly opposes the common view of gypsies and travellers as inherently *dis*honest and devious in their 'vagabond' lifestyles.

The nature of the 'mountain liberty' the poet reads in the faces of the Scottish drovers is not specified, but we can reasonably infer what it might mean to Clare. Romantic Scottishness was at its height in Britain in the 1820s, fed by the huge success of Sir Walter Scott's Waverley Novels, and all-too-vividly illustrated by the incident in which, 'be-kilted, be-sporraned, be-tartaned', the Prince Regent, garishly decked-out in Royal Stuart tartan and flesh-coloured tights, had paraded the streets of Edinburgh in 1822.[60] Clare knew the Waverley Novels, as is suggested by an untitled late poem which begins 'The heart of Midlothian is nearly my own', and

50

later mentions 'the sweet Lammermore'.[61] Scott's tragic story of 'The Two Drovers' came too late to influence the passage on Scottish drovers in *The Shepherd's Calendar* (both were published in 1827); but Clare may very well have read Scott's other great 'drover' text, *Rob Roy* (1817).[62]

The phrase itself, 'mountain liberty', gives a further clue. It echoes John Milton's personified figure of 'the mountain nymph Sweet Liberty' in his poem 'L'Allegro', line 36. Mountains were always interesting to Clare. They made an imaginative contrast with the flat fenland country in which even molehills were a welcome sight to the poet, and the modestly rising ground near Burghley was almost sublime.[63] Mountains are by their very nature un-enclosable, their only real agricultural use being to sustain small numbers of hardy, free-ranging sheep. They were never part of the enclosure movement, nor could they be. The unenclosed openness and 'liberty' of the Scottish mountains, and the apparently unbounded freedoms of the drovers, seen as they slowly pass through Clare's own landscape, come together with Clare's interest in the Scottish self-taught poets and ballad writers and the Waverley novels, with his own Scottish blood, and with the general English interest in Scotland of the period, to form an extremely powerful idea. Scotland becomes for Clare another kind of paradise, characterised as 'An Eden a' the year'.[64]

Modern readers will be more familiar with the idea of Scotland as England's romanticised 'other'.[65] But we should not dismiss Clare's Scottish dreams out of hand. Clearly they hold some potential for the expression of libertarian and anti-enclosure feelings, and there is evidence that Clare was

familiar with Scottish history, for example, the events of the
'45 Rebellion, and the earlier struggles of the Covenanters.[66]
There is a note of radicalism running through much of his
Scottish material. The ways Clare could directly challenge
the boundedness of his landscape and his society were
limited. But by writing into his poetry rebellious, unfearing
souls from the unenclosable mountains of a country with
strongly independent traditions, who seem to go where they
like, wear what they like; indeed whose very cattle, 'Wi cockd
up horns & curling crown / & dewlap bosom hanging down',
seem to mock the bland slabbiness of post-Bakewellian
English beasts, Clare turns the poetry itself into a means of
resistance. No wonder the shepherd, the mower, and even
the shepherd's dog, stop work and stare when the drovers
come by: by Clare's lights they are glimpsing Arcadia, and
freedom.

Clare is almost too close to the gypsies, too keenly aware of their hardship and the desperate improvisation their survival necessitates, to perceive them in this way with any consistency. Scotland and the Scots are, by their very remoteness and strangeness, more easily marshalled into a counter-cultural force. At its best, this works well, as when Clare considers Scotland obliquely, via its national emblem, in the poem 'The Thistle':

> I love the thistle and its prickles too
> Cobwebs are round it with a veil of dew
> I love the thistle where it bravely stands
> For rights of Liberty in many lands
> Simply defying every rogueish eye
> With 'wha dare meddle wi me' that passes bye
> My right is simple, blooming 'mong the flowers
> That God's hand scatters on this land of ours[67]

Scotland is not mentioned, but the personified thistle utters the well-known, defiant Scottish motto, 'Wha dare meddle wi me'. By using a symbol of Scotland rather than Scotland itself, Clare combines the characteristics of Scottish liberty with those of one of his other 'trespassers', the free-growing weed, the thistle.

The result is cleverly humorous. The poet's 'love' is expressed not only towards the aesthetic qualities of the thistle, the way it supports a beautifully be-dewed spider's web, but also towards its prickles, drawing attention to the fact that this is a rather well-armed weed, whose God-given right to live in liberty, exactly where it has been 'scattered', will be defended if needs be by force. Weeds, like common land, disordered hedgerows, bushes and briars, are the fuzzy bits in the margins of the enclosed landscape, the uncontrolled refuges of a natural tendency to disorderliness that Clare consistently praises in terms which suggest that natural anarchy can carry a political message about the human ordering of the landscape.[68] In the poem 'Solitude', the furze and briars, two more militantly well-armed weeds, are respectively 'unmolested' and 'by freedom sown'.[69] And in an untitled quatrain the weeds celebrate their freedom in a drunken dance, assisted by yet another 'trespasser', the wind:

> The weeds beside the hedge dance
>> Like so many drunken men,
> Then rest till breezes whisper,
>> Then up and dance agen[70]

Drunkenness is another kind of freedom, as Clare well knew. He describes it wonderfully and hilariously in his ballad 'The Cellar Door'.[71] Several men enjoy an unexpected interruption to their day-labour when a barrel of beer falls off a dray and they help to bring it into the bar. Obviously after this heavy work they must needs slake their thirst, and one good drink deserves another, as the carefree, workshy 'toper' firmly believes:

> & the toper who carried his house on his head
> No wife to be teazing no ba[i]rns to be fed
> Would sit out the week or the month or the year
> Or a lifetime so long as he'd credit or beer

As for his new workmen friends, the beer in them starts to talk with growing confidence:

> The ploughman he talked of his skill as divine
> How he could plough thurrows as straight as a line
> & the blacksmith he swore had he but the command
> He coud shoe the kings hunter the best in the land
> & the cobbler declared was his skill but once seen
> He should soon get an order for shoes for the queen[72]

In their moment of beer-fuelled joy, the pride these three workers feel in their respective crafts—which they have in fact just abandoned for the day—lifts them to the level of the 'divine', or at least, now feeling rather like royalty themselves, to imagine serving the king and queen with the products of their labour. These fairly respectable artisanal responses, in which labour is imaginatively replaced by its platonic ideal, contrast with that of the toper, whose joy leaves absolutely every responsibility behind save that of getting money for more beer. (There is a long digression about his delight in finding a long-lost 'stiver', or sixpence, in a fold of his trouser pocket, line 95.) In his affectionate depiction of a group of men suddenly faced with seemingly unlimited drink and a credible pretext for casting work aside, Clare transgressively defies the ruling ideologies of temperance and work-discipline.[73] His publishers and patrons often warned him about the perils of drinking too much. But 'The Cellar Door' puts two fingers up to the overseers of the underclass, and is still sung or recited today.[74]

To come back to the equally disorderly subject of weeds, in 'The Progress of Ryhme' Clare argues coherently against the very terminology by which weeds are marginalised:

& weeds that bloomed in summers hours
I thought they should be reckoned flowers
They made a garden free for all
& so I loved them great & small
& sung of some that pleased my eye
Nor could I pass the thistle by
But paused & thought it could not be
A weed in natures poesy
No matter for protecting wall
No matter though they chance to fall
Where sheep & cows & oxen lie[75]

The thistle is again central, the focus of Clare's argument for the significance of even the humblest representative of freedom. Here its sturdy independence represents an eloquent rejection of Clare's old enemy, the 'protecting wall', so necessary to enclosed, domesticated plants.

The stanza from 'The Thistle' shows the seemingly effortless way in which Clare could suggest deeper meanings in the simplest piece of natural observation. It is not suggested that he set out to write an elaborate piece of literary subversion here. The thistle's speech is a simple, humorous rendering of the stereotypical figure of the truculent, defiant Scotsman. The wider meaning emerges from Clare's first concern, which is always to capture the spirit of what he sees. A particular strength of Clare's poetry is its ability to make one see what he sees with great clarity (the lurking pun in his name is fortunate), while suggesting broader layers of significance. Gypsies and Scottish drovers have intrinsic interest as subjects of Clare's rural, descriptive poetry and prose. Yet he also manages to show how their itinerant lifestyles run counter to the repressive orderliness of the English countryside, offering alternative ways of life. The technique gives his writing a depth and a bite not often available in picturesque and pastoral writing.

5. Enclosure

Opposite stanza 107 in the manuscript of Clare's long, quasi-autobiographical early poem, 'The Village Minstrel', is a worried marginal note in the hand of his publisher John Taylor: 'This is radical Slang'.[76] Taylor's anxiety was no doubt fed by the agitation Clare's patron, Lord Radstock, felt about the political impulse in the poet's writing. Clare had written this:

> There once was lanes in natures freedom dropt
> There once was paths that every valley wound
> Inclosure came & every path was stopt
> Each tyrant fixt his sign where pads was found
> To hint a trespass now who crossd the ground
> Justice is made to speak as they command
> The high road now must be each stinted bound
> —Inclosure thourt a curse upon the land
> & tastless was the wretch who thy existence pland

Like many of his contemporaries, such as Lord Byron and Percy Shelley, Clare was an intensely political poet. And like his poetic forbears, Oliver Goldsmith and George Crabbe, the politics of his poetry focus especially on the rural world, and what Raymond Williams called the 'well-known habit of using the past... as a stick to beat the present'.[77] In Clare's view, however, Crabbe 'writes about the peasantry as much like the Magistrate as the Poet'. This comment occurs in a letter to a fellow self-taught poet, Allan Cunningham, and contrasts Crabbe unfavourably with a third self-taught poet, Robert Bloomfield, suggesting Clare is conscious of the effects of class on poets' views of rural life. Crabbe, he says, 'knows little or nothing' about the peasantry compared to Bloomfield, who 'not only lived amongst them, but felt and shared the pastoral pleasures with the peasantry of whom he sung'.[78]

For the peasantry and those poets who 'lived amongst them', the main issue of enclosure was not, as it had been for an early pro-enclosure poet like John Dyer, agricultural efficiency. It was trespass, the fearful presence lurking at the heart of stanza 107 and, for the 'peasant', the major conceptual creation of enclosure. At first the signs only 'hint' at trespass, but in the next line a real power of enforcement is evoked: 'Justice is made to speak as they command'. The land-enclosers have the magistracy in their pockets, and what that might mean to Clare can easily be imagined (especially remembering his bizarre encounter with the paranoid magistrate and the whistling hedger).

The problem is one of attitudes. Dyer had advocated enclosure to promote agricultural efficiency and to deter the 'idle pilf'rer' who too easily 'Eludes detection' under a common-field system. Similarly for Crabbe, the common land of the heath was agriculturally unproductive, and also the territory of 'lawless' pirates and smugglers (Crabbe was a coastal poet, brought up in Aldeburgh), 'Rank' weeds, and all manner of ugly—i.e. unproductive—vegetation. Thistles may be defiantly beautiful objects to Clare, as we have seen, but in Crabbe's world they actually constitute a threat to the nation's children: 'There thistles stretch their prickly arms afar, / And to the ragged infant threaten war'.[79] On the other hand the enclosers are 'tastless' for Clare, because they have 'stopt' the natural tracery of paths from which the countryside can be seen in a boundless variety of ways. The 'high road now must be each stinted bound'—the chopped-off sound of the word 'stinted' finely enunciates the meagreness of the new, restricted view. Beauty is, as always, both in the eye of the beholder and indicative of wider attitudes. For both Crabbe and Clare, the poetical and the political are inseparable. Political views are expressed in terms of views of the landscape: the view of a magistrate, or the view of a peasant; the view from the high road, or the view from the winding paths of freedom.

Clare's poetic war with enclosure, with its methodological contrasting of past and present, beauty and ugliness, single and multiple perspectives, was pursued through his early and middle period verse. Nowhere is it more strongly argued than in 'The Mores', a poem in which Clare summons substantial rhetorical powers, lifting his anxieties about trespass and enclosure into the greater tradition of English political protest writing, the tradition of Langland, Milton, Swift; Paine, Wollstonecraft and Cobbett. Here, 'trespass' is transformed into the much greater subject of civil rights, ownership and control.

In the earlier poem dealing with enclosure, 'The Lamentation of Round Oak Waters', Clare had addressed this local stream in a very personal way, in the tradition of telling one's sorrows to the waters.[80] A later poem, 'The Lament of Swordy Well', dramatically gives the land itself a voice, so that it can protest that at the present rate of plunder, 'My name will quickly be the whole / Thats left of Swordy Well'.[81] But in 'The Mores' the poet takes full and confident control of his narrative, telling it as if he were one of the village storytellers he so admired.[82]

The view that opens the poem offers grand perspectives:

> Far spread the moorey ground a level scene
> Bespread with rush & one eternal green
> That never felt the rage of blundering plough
> Though centurys wreathed springs blossoms on its
>   brow
> Still meeting plains that stretched them far away
> In uncheckt shadows of green brown & grey
> Unbounded freedom ruled the wandering scene
> Nor fence of ownership crept in between
> To hide the prospect of the following eye
> Its only bondage was the circling sky
> One mighty flat undwarfed by bush & tree
> Spread its faint shadow of immensity
> & lost itself which seemed to eke its bounds
> In the blue mist the orisons edge surrounds
>
>   (lines 1-14)[83]

This opening movement has an epic quality. Words like 'Far', 'eternal', 'centurys', and the sequence of negatives ('never felt', 'uncheckt', 'unbounded', 'undwarfed'), suggest immense scales of time and space. The language of unbounded vastness dominates. Clare sees freedom from agricultural enclosure in an almost painterly way, as freedom from picturesque composition. At the same time, the heavy use of past tenses, and the way in which negatives like 'unbounded' and 'undwarfed' include their opposites ('bounded', 'dwarfed'), strongly suggest the kinds of contrasts we have mentioned: past versus present, openness versus closure, large versus small. The key word is perhaps 'unbounded', and against this huge and heroic openness is set the villain of the piece, the 'fence of ownership' (still absent at this stage, though mentioned) that, like Satan in the garden of Eden, will soon have 'crept in between'. The characteristic openness of the fen country east of Helpston works to Clare's literary advantage, as he invokes the sublimity of the unbounded.

The second movement of the poem brings us sharply into the present:

> Now this sweet vision of my boyish hours
> Free as spring clouds & wild as summer flowers
> Is faded all—a hope that blossomed free
> & hath been once no more shall ever be
> Inclosure came & trampled on the grave
> Of labours rights & left the poor a slave
> & memorys pride ere want to wealth did bow
> Is both the shadow & the substance now
>
> (lines 15-22)

The opening lines acknowledge that Clare's position is a nostalgic one which associates freedom with happy memories of his own childhood. By doing so they strengthen the historical force of what follows, turning a familiar pastoral device into a powerful rhetoric. Lines 19-20 state the case against enclosure in strongly political language ('Inclosure came... & left the poor a slave'), and the final lines, like the opening lines of the passage, address 'external' politics through the 'internal' consciousness: 'And memorys pride ere want to wealth did bow / Is both the shadow & the substance now'. The proud and precious memory of 'unbounded freedom', of a time before the needs of the poor were rejected in the interests of the rich, now must serve as both the insubstantial reflection of that vision, and the only tangible evidence of it that remains. All the poor have left is pride in the nobility of their former vision. Clare's political protest is rhetorically enriched by this disillusioned and angry insistence that—even though pride in one's past is a real and important resource—the poor have been left to feed themselves on dreams.[84]

At this point Clare plunges us into his ideal past again:

> The sheep & cows were free to range as then
> Where change might prompt nor felt the bonds of men
> Cows went & came with every morn & night
> To the wild pasture as their common right
> & sheep unfolded with the rising sun
> Heard the swains shout & felt their freedom won
> Tracked the red fallow field & heath & plain
> Then met the brook & drank & roamed again
> The brook that dribbled on as clear as glass
> Beneath the roots then hid among the grass
> While the glad shepherd traced their tracks along
> Free as the lark & happy as her song   (lines 23-34)

He has returned to the 'sweet vision' for another look at it, and he will return to it again (in lines 51-64)—re-iteration is an important rhetorical technique. In this blissful scene, cattle, sheep, the shepherd, the lark and the stream are all equally free to wander where they will, claiming their 'common right'. While freedom of expression, the 'right to song', as Clare calls it elsewhere, is dramatically conveyed in the exuberant 'shout' of the swains, freedom of movement is portrayed as being available to all in this unenclosed landscape.

There are three 'speeches' against enclosure in the poem, at lines 15-22, 35-50, and 64-80; they get fiercer and more witheringly sarcastic. Here is the middle one, which dips repeatedly into what is lost, clashing the past and the present together to throw a discordant emphasis on the disastrous change that has occurred:

> But now alls fled & flats of many a dye
> That seemed to lengthen with the following eye
> Moors loosing from the sight far smooth & blea
> Where swopt the plover in its pleasure free
> Are vanished now with commons wild & gay
> As poets visions of lifes early day
> Mulberry bushes where the boy would run
> To fill his hands with fruit are grubbed & done
>
> (lines 35-42)

The last couplet shows this 'clashing' at its most effective. Through the boy's handfuls of mulberry fruit Clare deploys a favourite image in pastoral poetry, that of the fecundity and generous bounty of nature. We find it in Virgil's *Georgics* (II, 520) where 'Autumn drops her varied fruits at our feet', or in Andrew Marvell's poem 'Bermudas', where God 'makes the figs our mouths to meet / And throws the melons at our feet'. But then Clare does something entirely *unexpected* to the image: he dramatically smashes it with as tough a verbal club as he can find, the phrase 'grubbed & done', blunt monosyllables, emphatically set in the past tense, ugly, abrupt and final.

We now move out to the edges of the field, the common lands and woods that held such a fascination for Clare. But instead of pleasurable natural abundance, we find destruction and chaos:

> & hedgrow briars—flower lovers overjoyed
> Came & got flower pots—these are all destroyed
> & sky bound mores in mangled garbs are left
> Like mighty jiants of their limbs bereft   (lines 43-6)

The 'mighty jiants of their limbs bereft' suggest tree-felling and tree-lopping; it might also suggest fallen Gods (as in Keats's fragmentary 'Hyperion' poem, which Clare had read and praised).[85] Instead of natural abundance, and contrasting with the mutilated ugliness of the damaged trees, we now see the shaping of orderly small-mindedness, a truly *petit*-bourgeois landscape:

> Fence now meets fence in owners little bounds
> Of field & meadow large as garden grounds
> In little parcels little minds to please
> With men & flocks imprisoned ill at ease
> (lines 47-50)

Clare's repetition of 'little' is rather like that in Pete Seeger's song 'Little Boxes', a satire on a modern, semi-detached type of restricted horizon. Imprisonment is a favourite negative image in Clare's later poetry and, not surprisingly, it is used repeatedly in his letters home from the Northampton General Lunatic Asylum.[86] It is the epitome of claustrophobic 'littleness'. Against this restrictive 'littleness' of a bounded landscape Clare now sets a different and more positive sort of 'littleness', that of the minute diversity of unenclosed paths and flowers—just as in line 48 he gives a negative kind of largeness, one restricted to the size of a garden. These two uses of 'little' make an effective double contrast with the unboundedness of the early stanzas:

> Each little path that led its pleasant way
> As sweet as morning leading night astray
> Where little flowers bloomed round a varied host
> That travel felt delighted to be lost
> Nor grudged the steps that he had taen as vain
> When right roads traced his journeys end again
> Nay on a broken tree hed sit awhile
> To see the mores & fields & meadows smile
> Sometimes with cowslaps smothered—then all white
> With daiseys—then the summers splendid sight
> Of corn fields crimson oer the 'head ach' bloomd
> Like splendid armys for the battle plumed
> He gazed upon them with wild fancys eye
> As fallen landscapes from an evening sky
>
> (lines 51-64)

This third view of the pre-enclosure landscape is one Clare often uses, that of unrestrained wandering, the speaker happy to be 'astray' and 'delighting to be lost', refusing orderliness and purpose, enjoying a 'broken' tree, a riot of flowers. The last couplet changes the pace, moving the poem gently from a sense of celebration ('splendid armys') to a sense of loss ('fallen landscapes'), and an elegiac note in 'evening sky'. But just as one becomes attuned to this new mood—a familiar one in pastoral —the poet again does something purposely jarring, dramatically stopping the verse dead in the middle of a line with the appropriate word, 'stopt':

> These paths are stopt—the rude philistines thrall
> Is laid upon them & destroyed them all
> Each little tyrant with his little sign
> Shows where man claims earth glows no more divine
> On paths to freedom & to childhood dear
> A board sticks up to notice 'no road here'
> & on the tree with ivy overhung
> The hated sign by vulgar taste is hung
> As tho the very birds should learn to know
> When they go there they must no further go
>
> (lines 65-74)

Yet again we are brought back to destruction and restriction. The 'little tyrant' replaces the 'mighty jiants', and the transcendent 'glow' of the 'divine' is lost in the grubby claiming of each earthly patch. The continued repetition of 'little' emphasises a contrast between the little path and little flowers, attractive because of their unpretentiousness, and the little tyrants, unattractive because of their pretensions. The trespass notices that the 'tyrants' put up are condemned as spiritually destructive to the poet's ruling deities of nature ('earth'), childhood, and liberty, and then treated with mocking sarcasm.

In this penultimate movement of the poem, righteous anger is the central means of expression. In the last three lines here (71-74) Clare may well be thinking of the idea (familiar in his day) of teaching lower-class children to read merely as a means of teaching them obedience. For Clare, whose great struggle had been to acquire and use his literacy in the richest way, this would seem a particularly perverse misuse of the written word. The absurd idea of the birds having to learn where to stop by reading the trespass sign, expresses well a sense of language (and nature) being betrayed and misused.

The final movement of the poem is a little hard to decode:

> Thus with the poor scared freedom bade good bye
> And much the[y] feel it in the smothered sigh
> & birds & trees & flowers without a name
> All sighed when lawless laws enclosure came
> & dreams of plunder in such rebel schemes
> Have found too truly that they were but dreams
> (lines 75-80)

The obscurity in his meaning here may be a disguise behind which Clare could hide from being too outspoken on such radical matters. A deleted first draft indicates his drift much more clearly:

> For with the poor stern freedom bade farewell
> & fortune hunters totter w[h]ere they fell
> They dreamd of <wealth> riches in the rebel scheme
> & find too truly that they did but dream
> (Peterborough MS A18, p. 6)

The draft reveals that Clare is rounding off his poem with the bitter reflection that the destruction of physical and imaginative freedom by enclosure has benefitted neither the poor, who were robbed of their common rights, nor those who sought to gain by the scheme. The most revealing change between draft and fair copy is the smothering of the forthright line about 'fortune hunters', and its replacement with a more conventional sentimental line, that contains its own ironic comment on the smothering of a sigh at the loss of freedom. The additional new lines (77-78) bring in a third victim: nature.

In these final lines, Clare sums up and brings together the oppositions upon which the poem is built: freedom and enclosure, law and lawlessness, poverty and wealth, fact and dream, substance and shadow. The argument is now clear, and deals in successive couplets with the poor, nature, and those who have enclosed the land. The concept of freedom has been frightened away from any connection with the poor, who sigh at its loss. Nature, which shares the namelessness and powerlessness of the poor, also shares the regret and, as in conventional pastoral elegy, sighs alongside the human mourners at the loss. Finally, those who have caused this loss, the perpetrators of the 'lawless laws' of enclosure, must also share the disappointments of the poor. Where earlier the poor had found that they had only their 'memorys pride' as both shadow and substance, now the rich have discovered that their own dreams of plunder are just that: dreams. All, in fact, have lost, in this bitter and angry elegy for the pointless and calamitous loss of the divinity of earth.[87]

'The Mores' remains a classic of protest literature, and a fine poem. The power of its impassioned rhetoric, its mixture of righteous anger and elegiac sadness, its dramatic contrasts of time and space, set it alongside its major contemporaries, poems like Shelley's 'The Masque of Anarchy' and 'England in 1819', Byron's political verses, Ebenezer Elliott's 'Corn-Law Rhymes', and the later Chartist poets. It also bears comparison with the great political prose writings and speech-writing of its age, an age of dramatic political change. It is an evocative and timely response to the changes of enclosure, one which sets out the arguments against the enclosure movement's strengthening of private property laws, with their attendant concept of trespass, appropriately and with great rhetorical skill and emotional energy.[88]

Conclusion: The art behind Clare's artlessness

When Barbara Strang wrote her study of Clare's language, she tended to count usages and make tables of frequencies. It seemed a tedious way of looking at poetry, and yet she had a genius for making interesting observations out of the driest detail. When it came to frequencies of words, she noticed that counting was not enough. Clare's 'fondness for near-synonymous variants' meant that words had to be grouped in a network of interlinked clusters. For example, she listed the following groups (from Clare's 1835 volume, *The Rural Muse*):

'memory' e. g., words like memory, recollection, forget
'past' e. g., words like past, old, ancient
'continuity and change' e. g., words like eternity, immortal, new fangled
'unprocessed' (as a desirable state) e. g., words like unbroken, unchangeable, undisturbed
'paradise lost' e.g., words like eden, emparadised, lose
'threatened joy' e.g., words like joy, rapture, fear, danger, loss
'the concealed, the great in the small' e.g., words like little, hid(den)[89]

These words cluster in groups around particular ideas, and also connect with each other; and this is entirely characteristic of Clare's poetry. Memory (the first group) takes one into the past (the second group) to consider continuity and change (the third group). There, Clare gives primacy to the next group, the 'unprocessed'—the changeless, the undisturbed things that remind us of Eden (like birds' nests). Paradise is lost, joy threatened (as nests are often threatened), following the patterns of Professor Strang's next two groups. But 'the concealed'—the hidden, the secret, the small, remain. 'The Mores' works in this way, though its downbeat ending excludes the saving virtues of 'the concealed': the ambiguous powers of memory and dreams are its only consolatory images. Many of Clare's poems follow this sort of pattern. The subtle and subdued connections Clare makes between these kinds of groups and ideas are one of the great strengths of his work, a continuous sub-text that weaves together apparently disparate materials, and brings into the close descriptiveness of his rural poetry metaphorical, political and philosophical meaning.

We want to suggest that the same thing happens when one looks at the ideas surrounding trespass: the word and the idea become enriched with metaphorical significance and provide an intellectual and literary coherence beneath the apparently clear surface of Clare's poetry. (Trespass specifically ties in with the particular clusters of words listed above, in that the longed-for Paradise is in one aspect the noble park, the land of the lord.) Trespass is related to concepts like ownership, enclosure, destruction of freedoms, ambition, class; it is set against the common (in both senses), the free, the gypsy, the wild, the careless.[90]

It is no longer enough to read Clare as a simple observer of nature in transparent descriptive verse, though it is his skill to appear to be an exact and innocent eye. We need to recognise that he works through groups of linked ideas, and through an instinctive ability to root his abstract thoughts in images that give consistency and solidity to his achievement. The idea of trespass, reaching out to its associated ideas and images, focuses one such group. It is a key concept in his writing, and in his imaginative world.

Notes

Epigraphs: *John Clare: By Himself*, ed. Eric Robinson and David Powell (Manchester and Ashington, 1996), p. 222; Chris Wood, from his song 'Mad John', Trespasser (RUF, 2007, RUFCD11).

1 *By Himself*, pp. 10-11. Clare's quotation from *The Seasons* (Spring, 1-4) is substantively accurate, but sufficiently variant in spelling and accidentals to show that he is quoting from memory. For a variant account of this episode in Clare's life see Mark Storey, 'Edward Drury's "Memoir" of Clare', *John Clare Society Journal* (*JCSJ*), 11 (1992), 14-16.

2 Clare says he 'nestled in a lawn' inside the wall, suggesting inviolable, womb-like safety, something he often finds in secluded natural spaces, for example 'In Hilly Wood', where he remarks how 'sweet it is to be thus nestling deep in boughs' (*Early Poems*, II, p. 62).

3 Getting out of sight in order to be able to read and write is an expedient Clare repeated. When he worked 'in the Farmers Gardens', he writes, 'I usd to drop down behind a hedge bush or dyke and write down my things upon the crown of my hat' (*By Himself*, p. 78).

4 Many of Clare's poems, however, celebrate Sunday as a day of freedom, especially during 'church time', though dodging services often earned him a 'strong snubbing', as he puts it. 'On Sundays I generally stole from my Companions whose Manners and Play was noways Agreable to me and sholld into the Woods Where I was most happy as I always lovd to be by myself' (*By Himself*, p. 27). See also 'Sunday', *The Early Poems of John Clare*, ed. Eric Robinson and David Powell (Oxford, 1989), Volume II, pp. 359-62; 'Sabbath Walks', *Early Poems*, II, p. 385; 'A Sunday with Shepherds and Herdboys', *Poems of the Middle Period 1822-1837*, II, ed. Eric Robinson, David Powell and P.M.S. Dawson (Oxford, 1996), 15-20; 'In the Field', *The Later Poems of John Clare*, ed. Eric Robinson and David Powell (Oxford, 1984), II, pp. 839-40.

5 Compare: 'What, know you not, / Being mechanical, you ought

not walk / Upon a labouring day without the sign / Of your profession?' (Shakespeare, *Julius Caesar*, I, i, 1-5).

6 *The Prelude: A Parallel Text*, ed. J.C. Maxwell, rev. ed. (Harmondsworth, 1972), p. 54 (lines 388-9 in 1805, 361-2 in 1850).

7 For a contemporary exploration of the continuing significance of the creative transgressiveness Clare employs, see the 2016 show by the comedian and activist Mark Thomas, entitled 'Trespass'. In this show he takes the tradition of the 1930s ramblers into the city and 'sets out to try and carve a small space in the urban world where mischief and random chance can lurk' (*ON: Nottingham Lakeside Arts, Dec 2014-Mar 2016* (publicity pamphlet, Nottingham, 2016), p. 46).

8 'After Hearing Rural Ryhmes of W. H. Praisd by a Lady', *Early Poems*, II, pp. 323-4, line 8.

9 John Lucas writes: 'Trespasser, fugitive, outlaw: these are the kinds of conditions, the forms of experience, which Clare addresses in his many poems about birds and animals.' (*England and Englishness: Ideas of Nationhood in English Poetry 1688-1900* (London, 1990), p. 151).

10 See 'Ballad' ('Boys bring the booty from the cave') and 'Robin Hood & The Gamekeepers A Ballad', *Poems of the Middle Period IV*, ed. Eric Robinson, David Powell and P. M. S. Dawson (Oxford, 1998), pp. 395-97, 422-30.

11 For more on Clare's relationship to Thomson and eighteenth-century topographical poetry see John Barrell, *The Idea of Landscape and the Sense of Place 1730-1840: An Approach to the Poetry of John Clare* (London, 1972).

12 Margaret Grainger and John Chandler, 'From Helpston to Burghley: A Reading of Clare's "Narrative Verses"', *JCSJ*, 7 (1988), 26-40, p. 34.

13 *Early Poems*, II, pp. 4-10; for convenience we add the verse numbers used in Grainger and Chandler's text, *JCSJ*, 8 (1977), 27-32. The poem was first published in *The Village Minstrel* (1821). Clare's 'echo' here itself echoes John Dyer's popular poem, 'The Country Walk', especially Dyer's lines: 'Tis but the Eccho stays behind' (71) and 'See her Woods, where Ecchoe talks' (114). In

2014 a sound and image installation by the artist Ainsley Hillard at Dyer's birthplace, Aberglasney, where the poem was written, drew on this last phrase for its title, 'Where Echo Talks'.

14 The phrase 'gleaming rapterous on my sight' is redolent of some of the phrases Bunyan uses to indicate a shining, gleaming quality to the heavenly city and its inhabitants, in the closing chapter of *Pilgrim's Progress*. The language of the last four lines of stanza 11 suggests a source in one of the many eighteenth-century poems on the theme of *concordia discors*, for example Pope's *Windsor Forest*, lines 11-16:

> Here Hills and Vales, the Woodland and the Plain,
> Here Earth and Water seem to strive again,
> Not Chaos-like together crush'd and bruis'd,
> But as the World, harmoniously confus'd:
> Where Order in Variety we see,
> And where, tho' all things differ, all agree.

(Grainger and Chandler suggest Pope's 'Order in Variety' as a potential point of comparison; *JCSJ*, 7 (1988), 35 and note); *The Poems of Alexander Pope*, ed. John Butt (London, 1963), p. 195.

15 Although Clare generally uses words like 'liberty', 'free' and 'freedom' straightforwardly, he shows awareness in poems like 'The Fallen Elm', of a more cynical, self-interested kind of 'freedom', which he characterises as 'the cant term of enslaving tools / To wrong another by the name of right' (*Poems of the Middle Period III*, ed. Eric Robinson, David Powell and P.M.S. Dawson (Oxford, 1998), p. 440).

16 As noted by Margaret Grainger, *JCSJ*, 8 (1987), 33. We are much indebted to this excellent essay on the poem by Grainger and Chandler, which traces Clare's route and provides a map.

17 'The Progress of Ryhme', *Middle Period III*, pp. 492-503 (498).

18 An untitled poem ('Where the deer with their shadows passed swifter than thought', *Later Poems*, II, p. 1107), dated 1842-54, shows Burghley was remembered in the asylum period:

> Ye green shades of Burghley! how lovely you seem,
> Your sweet spreading oaks and your braken so green,
> Your green plots as sweet as a shepherd boy's dream,
> 'Neath the shade of dark trees where I've many a day been,

And sitting in braken or roots of the lime,
Amusing my leisure in ballads and rhyme. (lines 5-10)

19 'The Journal, Saturday 16 April 1825', *By Himself*, p. 222. See p. 100 for a similar incident.

20 J.L. and Barbara Hammond, *The Village Labourer*, Vol. I (London, 1911), pp. 183-97; Harry Hopkins, *The Long Affray: the Poaching Wars in Britain* (London, 1985). For a useful short summary see Pamela Horn, *The Rural World 1780-1850: Social Change in the English Countryside* (London, 1980), pp. 171-83. On the eighteenth-century background to this conflict see the two essays by Douglas Hay in *Albion's Fatal Tree: Crime and Society in Eighteenth century England*, eds. Hay, Linebaugh et al (London, 1975); E.P. Thompson, *Whigs and Hunters: The Origins of the Black Act* (London, 1975).

21 Clare himself was never a poacher, though he describes them in the poem 'The Poachers', unpublished in his lifetime. See *Middle Period IV*, pp. 378-9.

22 *By Himself*, pp. 74-5.

23 *Poems of the Middle Period V*, ed. Eric Robinson, David Powell and P.M.S. Dawson (Oxford, 2003), p. 288.

24 Neil Philip, 'To John Clare', *JCSJ*, 5 (1986), 36.

25 ('I Saw a Tree with Cheries Red'), *Early Poems*, I, pp. 513-4. Robinson and Powell write (p. 581): 'As Clare was using this cypher-book from the age of ten these two arithmetical poems may be his earliest attempts at rhyme.' (The other poem, in a similar vein, concerns a maypole). It seems likely that Clare invented or possibly learned these riddles as part of the process of learning geometry described in *By Himself*, p. 7.

26 Clare-Taylor, January-February 1832, i, *The Letters of John Clare*, ed. Mark Storey (1985), pp. 568-9. This is one of several drafts of a letter to Taylor, following a period of heightened tension between the two men over the fact that Clare's income remained tied up.

27 'Autumn', *Natural History Prose Writings*, pp. 335-6. Grainger dates this piece, which is in Northampton MS 6, to Autumn/Winter 1841, which was, as Grainger puts it, 'the respite between the two periods of incarceration'.

28 'Autumn', p. 336.

29 *Middle Period V*, p. 215.

30 *Natural History Prose Writings*, p. 317.

31 *Middle Period IV*, p. 149.

32 *Middle Period V*, pp. 359-60 (360).

33 'The Mores', *Middle Period II*, pp. 247-50 (349), lines 72 and 70, discussed in detail later.

34 Middleton Murry, for example, argues that Clare has purity of vision. He writes: 'It is hard to imagine that the poet... who could express what he saw with an ease and naturalness such that the expression strikes as part of the very act of seeing... should ever have thought, or should ever have had the impulse to think, about what he saw.' John Barrell quotes this, and appears to agree with him and with Donald Davie's similar view, when he writes: 'Davie's point is relevant here too, that Clare's language refuses to let us look beyond the things and actions he names, to anything analogous.' But part of what we are saying in this essay is that Clare's poems often insist on being understood in more ways than simply the literal. (Barrell goes on to offer a more nuanced view of Clare's descriptive clarity. He also comments briefly on the poem under discussion here. See *The Idea of Landscape*, pp. 122, 130-1, 142-3.)

35 'A Sunday with Shepherds and Herdboys' (*Middle Period II*, pp. 15-20) is especially interesting in this respect, suggesting a range of illicit activities. Gypsies and stolen peas are also brought together in poems such as 'The Hollow Tree', *Middle Period IV*, p. 298, and 'Fairy Things: Swordy Well', *Middle Period II*, pp. 115-16.

36 Clare writes of the gypsies: 'I usd to spend my sundays and summer evenings among them learning to play the fiddle in their manner by the ear and joining in their pastimes of jumping dancing and other amusments' (*By Himself*, p. 83).

37 See the 'Journey out of Essex', *By Himself*, pp. 257-65. Andrew Kötting's recent film *By Our Selves* (2015) is concerned with this event in Clare's life.

38 *Middle Period IV*, 52-56 (52).

39 'October', *Poems of the Middle Period I*, ed. Eric Robinson, David Powell and P.M.S. Dawson (Oxford, 1996), p. 139 (lines 44-6).

40 As well as the texts quoted see, for example, 'The Gypsies Evening Blaze', *Early Poems*, I, p. 33; 'Reccolections after a Ramble', *Early Poems*, II, pp. 187-96, lines 49-50 ('The gypsey tune was loud & strong / As round the camp they dancd a gig').

41 'The Gipseys Camp', lines 17-22, *Early Poems*, II, pp. 119-20. Further references to gypsy fortune-telling occur in 'The Dissapointment', *Early Poems*, II, pp. 353-9, line 65; 'The Cross Roads or Haymakers Story', *Early Poems*, II, pp. 619-29, lines 45-6; 'The Village Minstrel', *Early Poems*, II, pp. 123- 79, stanzas 115-7, and *By Himself*, p. 85.

42 *By Himself*, p. 37.

43 'The Village Minstrel', *Early Poems*, II, pp. 123-79, stanza 113 (p. 171); 'The Gipsy Camp', *Later Poems*, I, p. 29, line 4.

44 *Middle Period V*, p. 375.

45 *Middle Period V*, p. 354.

46 'Song' ('Theres a wide spreading heath and its crowds of furze bushes', *Later Poems*, I, pp. 537-8), lines 10-11. There are other romantic or erotic gypsy poems in the *Later Poems*, including 'The Gipsey Lass', I, pp. 634-5; 'My Love She Was a Gypsey O', II, pp. 787-8; 'Sweet Sophy's Eyes are Chrystals Clear', II, p. 789; 'The Bonny Gipsey', II, pp. 866-7; 'Fly to the Forest My Susan', II, pp. 1057-8 (line 24); 'My Own Sweet Gipsey Girl', II, pp. 1096-7.

47 As well as political censorship to Clare's poetry, his bawdy writings were also suppressed. His patron, Lord Radstock, pressurised him over the poems 'My Mary' and 'Dolly's Mistake', and both were omitted from the third edition of *Poems Descriptive*, to Clare's frustration. See *Early Poems*, I, pp. 567, 582; Tim Chilcott, *A Publisher and His Circle* (London, Boston MA, 1972), pp. 92-3; J.W. and Ann Tibble, *John Clare, a Life* (London, 1972), p. 141; Clare-Hessey, ?10 July 1820, *Letters*, pp. 83-4. Sexual expression, and the social restrictions that inhibit it as a theme in Clare's writings, may perhaps also be seen as illustrating the theme of 'trespass' within the politics of Clare's texts' production. Indeed, what we might more broadly term 'sexual trespass' is a theme in Clare's work that is worth further consideration, though the evidence is less abundant than that of land trespass. Much material concerning, or addressed to, Mary Joyce, in particular,

suggests a feeling that Clare was seen as 'trespassing' in his love for her. (See especially the two passages grouped together as 'Memorys of Love' in *By Himself*, pp. 87-92; also 111-12.) For the parallel censorship of erotic passages in Keats's 'The Eve of St Agnes', see *Keats, The Complete Poems*, ed. John Barnard (second edition, 1977), pp. 619-20.

48 *Early Poems*, II, p. 250, lines 9-15.
49 'A Sunday with Shepherds and Herdboys', *Middle Period II*, pp. 15-20 (p. 20), line 162.
50 For the Game and Trespass Laws, see note 20.
51 'Going to the Fair', *Middle Period III*, pp. 91-118 (98), ll. 141-52. There are some other 'Dobbin' poems, notably 'The Death of Dobbin', *Early Poems*, I, pp. 84-90.
52 *By Himself*, pp. 83.
53 *By Himself*, p. 127. On Clare and whistling, see John Lucas and Allan Chatburn, *A Brief History of Whistling* (Nottingham: Five Leaves, 2013), pp. 34-5, 38-9, 80-83, 102-3.
54 'The Progress of Ryhme', *Middle Period III*, pp. 492-503 (494), line 80.
55 *By Himself*, p. 2.
56 Allan Ramsay (1684-1758) was the son of a lead mine manager, Robert Fergusson (1750-74) a clerk, Robert Burns (1759-96) the son of a cottar, James Hogg (1770-1835) a shepherd, Robert Tannahill (1774-1810) a weaver, Allan Cunningham (1784-1842) the son of a gardener and land agent. He made specific comments on most of the writers mentioned. Some indication of Clare's interests in Scottish culture is also given by the contents of his library. He owned two copies of Burns's Works (one presented by Sir Walter Scott), and at least four editions of texts by Cunningham (one presented by the author). He was given Fergusson's Poems in 1837, and owned five editions of works by Hogg, two editions of Ramsay's poems (an early interest), and Tannahill's *Poems & Songs Chiefly in the Scottish Dialect* (1817). His copy of Scott's *The Lady of the Lake* was presented by the author, and he also owned Scott's novel *Peveril of the Peak* (1822) and *Paul's Letters to His Kinfolk* (1817). Other texts by Scottish poets in his library include James Beattie's *The Minstrel* (2 copies)

and *The Wreath*, and, as discussed above, Thomson's *Seasons* (1818 edition). Also in his library are Robert Pollok's *Tales of the Covenanters* (1833) and John Wilson's *Light and Shadows of Scottish Life* (1824). See 'Clare's Library', [David Powell], *Catalogue of the John Clare Collection in the Northampton Public Library* (Northampton, 1964), items 112-14, 134-5, 171-4, 204, 244-8, 333, 340-1, 350-2, 372, 377, 401.

57 'July', *Middle Period 1*, 91-92.

58 The game laws highlighted being abroad 'at night' as a serious indication of illicit activity, especially where two or more were involved. See the Hammonds, as cited in note 18.

59 ('O'er Scotland's vales and mountains high'), *Later Poems*, I, pp. 478-9, lines 23-4.

60 J.H. Plumb, *The First Four Georges* (1956, 1966), p. 175.

61 ('The heart of Midlothian is nearly my own'), *Later Poems*, II, p. 888. Scott's *The Heart of Midlothian* was published in 1818, *The Bride of Lammermoor* in 1819. We have no further evidence, however, that Clare had read these novels.

62 Clare's maternal uncle was a drover, who kindled the eleven-year-old Clare's interest in poetry by bringing him an illustrated edition of 'Pomfrets Poems' from London. Drovers were a major source of information of all kinds in the eighteenth and nineteenth century. See Mark Storey, 'Edward Drury's "Memoir" of Clare', *JCSJ*, 11 (1992), 14-16.

63 Clare tells the painter Rippingille: 'you know our scenery our highest hills are molehills & our best rocks are the edges of stonepits' (Clare-Rippingille, 14 May 1826, *Letters*, p. 379).

64 'Scotland', *Later Poems*, II, p. 690, line 8.

65 This is a theme in John McGrath's recently-revived play about modern Scotland, *The Cheviot, the Stag and the Black, Black Oil*.

66 An allusion to Lord Balmerinos, one of the executed rebel lords of the '45 Rebellion, suggests Clare knew something of eighteenth-century Scottish history. He was given a copy of Robert Pollok's *Tales of the Covenanters* (1833) in 1834. See Clare-William Robertson, 29 January 1830, *Letters*, p. 497, and note 52, above.

67 'The Thistle', *Later Poems*, I, pp. 492-3, stanza 2.

68 Clare's interest in marginal and uncontrolled spaces foreshadows modern thinking on the importance of margins and of uncultivated, common and 'waste' land, seen for example in the work of Richard Mabey (*The Unofficial Landscape*, 1973; *The Common Ground*, 1980, *Weeds*, 2010), and in Marion Shoard's concept of 'Edgeland' (see the 2002 essay of this title on her webpage, www.marionshoard.co.uk).

69 'Solitude', *Early Poems*, II, pp. 338-52, lines 69, 71.

70 [Fragments], *The Poems of John Clare*, ed. J. W. Tibble (1935), II, p. 302.

71 Other verses about drinking include 'Song: come push round the glass tis a god in disguise' and 'The Topers Rant', *Middle Period*, IV, 61-2, 75-8, and 'Billings sorrow in being sober for want of money to get drunk', *Middle Period*, II, 76-7.

72 *Middle Period IV*, pp. 123-30 (129), lines 131-40.

73 On work-discipline, see E.P. Thompson, *Customs in Common* (London, 1991), 352-403.

74 The folk musician Pete Shaw has performed the poem on a number of occasions, including at his annual Clare Festival folk evenings in The Blue Bell in Helpston.

75 'The Progress of Ryhme', *Middle Period III*, pp. 492-503 (495), lines 84-95.

76 Taylor-Clare, 6 January 1821, *Letters*, p. 135. Thanks are due to Dr Robert Heyes for identifying the handwriting as being Taylor's, rather than Radstock's, as most sources state.

77 Raymond Williams, *The Country and the City* (London, 1985), p. 12. See also pp. 132-41.

78 Clare-Cunningham, 9 September 1824, *Letters*, p. 302.

79 John Dyer, *The Fleece* (London, 1757), II, pp. 127-8; George Crabbe, *The Village* (London, 1783), I, pp. 69-70.

80 *Early Poems*, I, 228-9.

81 *Middle Period V*, 105.

82 On this topic, see John Goodridge, *John Clare and Community* (Cambridge, 2013), chapter 8.

83 'The Mores', *Middle Period II*, pp. 347-50.

84 Thanks to Professor Claire Lamont for her thoughts on these lines. John Barrell (*The Idea of Landscape*, p. 199) reads 19-22

carefully, and concludes: '[the] poem seems to suggest (as far as I can understand the second couplet here) that the proud nostalgia for a lost independence—master and man—is all the property of the labourer now: and that in fact that nostalgia is the myth by which the labourer is able to hang on to some of his lost dignity.'

85 Clare-Hessey, ?10 July 1820; on Keats see Goodridge, *Clare and Community*, pp. 69-10.

86 For imprisonment imagery in the poetry see, inter alia, 'Expectation', *Early Poems I*, 353-4; ('Thrice Welcome to thy song sweet warbling thrush'), *Early Poems*, I, 515, ll, 11-14; and in *Later Poems*: 'Child Harold', I, 40-88, lines 77-80, 145-9, 241-5, 1022-3; 'Don Juan', I, 89-101, lines 179, 231-2, 270; 'The Skylark', I, 315, line 1; 'Song To his Wife', I, 344, lines 13-16; 'A Regret', I, 373, lines 1-5; 'Written in Prison', II, 1023-4. For prison references in the asylum period, see also *Letters*, pp. 645-7, 650, 654, 660-1, 664-6, 669, 673, 675, 678-9.

87 We should like to acknowledge invaluable advice on the text of this passage from the late David Powell; see also P.M.S. Dawson, 'John Clare—Radical?', *JCSJ*, 11 (1992), 17-27.

88 For recent comment on Clare's enclosure poems, see Robert Heyes, review of Simon White's *Romanticism and the Rural Community* (2013), *Romanticism*, 21, no. 3 (October 2015), 319-21.

89 Barbara Strang, 'John Clare's Language', in *The Rural Muse, Poems by John Clare*, ed. R.K.R. Thornton (Ashington and Manchester, 1982), p. 167.

90 poems about 'Careless' wanderings include 'Carless Rambles', *Middle Period IV*, p. 263.

Further reading on John Clare

The standard library edition of Clare's poetry, used in this essay, is the Oxford English Texts edition, edited by Eric Robinson, David Powell and others, published in nine volumes between 1984 and 2003 and divided into *Early Poems* (I-II), *Poems of the Middle Period* (I-V), and *Later Poems* (I-II). Oxford University Press has also published standard editions of some of Clare's prose: *Natural History Prose Writings* (1983), *Autobiographical Writings* (1983) and *Letters* (1985). Much prose remains unpublished, with major manuscript collections in Peterborough, Northampton and New York.

There are now a number of good and relatively affordable paperback selections of Clare, of which the best value for money is probably *John Clare: Major Works* (Oxford), followed by four of the Carcanet Press volumes: *The Midsummer Cushion* (1990), Clare's best selection of his own poetry; *John Clare: By Himself* (1996), which includes all his autobiographical writings and journals and supersedes the *Autobiographical Writings* mentioned above; *A Champion for the Poor* (2000), a generous selection of his radical and political poetry and prose; and Tim Chilcott's dual-text edition of *The Shepherd's Calendar* (2006), Clare's most important single poem (or rather sequence of poems). There is more dual-text work in Chilcott's edition of Clare's 1841 writings: *The Living Year* (Trent Editions, 1999). There is a paperback selection of the letters from Oxford (1990), who also offer a handsome and well-prepared edition of *The Shepherd's Calendar* (2014). The Penguin Classics (ed. Geoffrey Summerfield) and Faber selections (ed. Jonathan Bate, and a smaller edition ed. Paul Farley) can also be recommended.

These are lightly punctuated by the editors, whereas a great many modern Clare editions are printed 'raw' from his manuscripts. The John Clare Society has published two selections, *The Wood is Sweet* and *This Happy Spirit*, which are inexpensive, accessible and beautifully illustrated by the artist Carry Akroyd (there are many other Clare-inspired artworks on her website, www.carryakroyd.co.uk). The Everyman selection of Clare (ed. R.K.R. Thornton, 1997) is the best of the economy editions, and is now used to teach Clare in UK schools.

Much useful material may be found online, including Simon Sanada's editions of Clare's four lifetime volumes: these are on Simon Kövesi's 'John Clare' web page. Roger Rowe's 'John Clare Blog' offers an ever-changing selection of poems, images and comment. John Goodridge's 'John Clare Resources' page includes a year-by-year index of critical work on Clare from 1970, and a first-line index of Clare's poetry, and there is also Clare material on Goodridge's 'academia.edu' page.

The John Clare Society also has a web page; additionally, all are welcome to visit the Society's free, annual John Clare Festival in Helpston, usually held on the weekend nearest Clare's birthday, July 13th. (You can also join the Clare Society for a modest £15 a year, which gives access to three good newsletters a year and an annual journal that is one of the best of its kind.) There is also a John Clare Facebook group. The John Clare Trust and the Langdyke Trust have a special interest in conserving, respectively, Clare's cottage, and his countryside.

Although there is earlier critical work worth seeking out (especially the work of Edmund Blunden, and J.W. and Ann Tibble), modern critical debates about John Clare really began with John Barrell's book *The Idea of Landscape and the Sense of Place* (1972). There is useful information in Greg Crossan's *A Relish for Eternity* (1976), though this book is hard to find now. There were several fine studies in the 1980s, of which those of Tim Brownlow (*John Clare and Picturesque Landscape*, 1983), Tim Chilcott ('*a real world and doubting mind*', 1985) and Johanne Clare (*John Clare and the Bounds of Circumstance*, 1987) offer a range of approaches and critical ideas. Three essay collections were published in 1994 to mark Clare's bicentenary the previous year: *The Independent Spirit: John Clare and the Self-Taught Tradition*; *John Clare: a Bicentenary Celebration*, and *John Clare in Context*. These are listed and their contents detailed on the 'John Clare Resources' web page, along with a further collection published in 2000, *John Clare: New Approaches*. Ronald Blythe's *Talking About John Clare* (Trent Editions, 1999) is an accessible collection of talks and essays, now superseded by a larger collection, *At Helpston: Meetings with John Clare* (Black Dog, 2011). Since the millennium there has been a series of valuable studies, notably by Roger Sales (*John Clare: A Literary Life*, 2002), Alan Vardy (*John Clare, Politics and Poetry*, 2003), Paul Chirico (*John Clare and the Imagination of the Reader*, 2007), Mina Gorji (*John Clare and the Place of Poetry*, 2009), Sarah Houghton-Walker (*John Clare's Religion*, 2009), and John Goodridge (*John Clare and Community*, 2013, paperback 2015). Stephanie Kuduk Weiner's *Clare's Lyric: John Clare and Three Modern Poets* (Oxford, 2014) is a comparative study, putting Clare alongside Arthur Symons, Edmund Blunden and the American poet John Ashbery. Published in 2015 was *New Essays on John Clare: Poetry, Culture and Community*, ed. Simon Kövesi and Scott

McEathron (Cambridge UP), a rich and up-to-date collection, and due in 2016 is M.M. Mahood's *John Clare Flora* (Trent Editions), a useful and very readable reference book.

As for Clare's life, his own life-writing is perhaps the most rewarding starting point, as collected in *John Clare: By Himself*. The Jonathan Bate biography of 2003 supersedes all others in terms of accuracy and range of information, but each of the main biographies has its particular strengths. These range from Frederick Martin's lively 1865 account, to Roger Sales's deeply-contextualised 'life and works' study of 2003. The other main biographies are by J.L. Cherry (1873), J.W. and Anne Tibble (1932, revised 1972; their critical book on Clare of 1956 is also worth looking into); June Wilson (*Green Shadows*, 1951), and Edward Storey (*A Right to Song*, 1981).